# INTRODUCTION

**H**ow many times have you tried to draw something but then got discouraged and threw it away? This has happened to all of us, but it doesn't have to be that way. Many talented young cartoonists give up too quickly because they don't know how to get to the next level. That's where I come in.

*Christopher Hart's Cartoon Studio* will show you not only how to draw cool cartoon characters, but how to *think* about drawing so you can turn an okay cartoon into a great one. You'll learn the secrets of drawing funny cartoon characters, expressions, body types, personalities, costumes, and more. You'll draw animals as well as people. And you'll learn how to answer the question I'm asked most by young artists: How do you draw a character in different poses and make it look the same?

Once you've started drawing great characters, you'll want to do something with them, like put them in a comic strip. But how do you do that? Where do you place the characters? How do you make it look good?

Yep, you guessed it. That's where I come in again. This book will show you how to create funny comic strips, and I've even included a bunch of jokes for you to draw.

Drawing is like a magic trick—once you know the secret, you never forget it, and your family and friends will think it's cool. You don't need a deck of cards for these tricks, just a pencil, a piece of paper, and your imagination.

Enough said. Roll up your sleeves. And remember—you can do it!

CHRISTOPHER HART

# HOW TO DRAW THE CARTOON HEAD

**H**eads should be easy to draw. We see them all the time. Most of us have one. But the head can be a tricky piece of business.

Here's a system that will have you drawing great-looking cartoon heads without guessing. I call it the "circle and jaw technique." Add it to your bag of tricks and you'll be drawing heads in no time.

## THE CIRCLE AND JAW TECHNIQUE

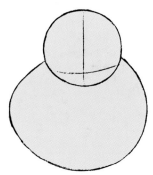

**1** *Start with the basic shape of the head. Draw it in two sections: a circle, which is the skull; and the jaw, which is, well, the jaw. Let's draw two guidelines through the circle. These will help you place features like the eyes and nose later.*

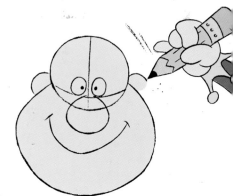

**2** *The bridge of the nose goes where the guidelines meet. The eyes rest on top of the horizontal guideline. The ears are drawn at the same height as the horizontal guideline. The mouth goes wherever you want—as long as it's below the nose.*

**3** *Now for the details! Add eyebrows and hair, and make the smile fancier with dimples or creases. Add the lower lip and chin.*

**4** *If you follow these steps, you won't have to worry about what goes where. Many artists use step-by-step methods to create their famous cartoon stars.*

# DRAWING HEADS FROM SIMPLE SHAPES

| PICK A SHAPE | FIND THE SKULL IN THE SHAPE | ADD THE GUIDELINES AND START PLACING THE FEATURES | FILL IN MORE FEATURES AND DETAILS | FINISH UP! |
|---|---|---|---|---|

Another way to draw heads is to start with a single shape. Simple shapes result in simple characters. To create more complex characters, like the rich lady shown here, just make a small change to a simple shape. (I changed the shape of an oval for the rich lady's head.) Be careful not to make the shape too complicated.

# CARTOON HEAD TILTS

The two questions I'm most often asked when I give demonstrations are, "How do you draw a character in different poses and still make it look the same?" and "Did your wife let you out of the house wearing that tie?" Hey—I *like* this tie, okay? Now to answer the first question:

You too will want to draw your character in many positions. After all, cartoon characters don't just stand still. Begin by imagining the skull as a basketball. Draw two guidelines on it. Where the two lines meet is where the bridge of the nose will go. This point also shows you *the direction that the face will point.*

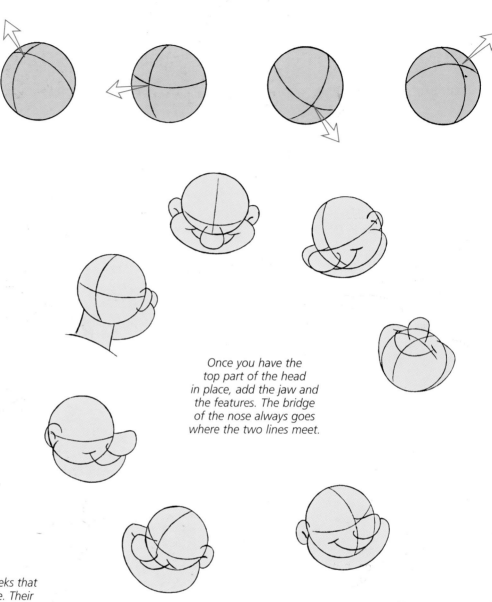

*Once you have the top part of the head in place, add the jaw and the features. The bridge of the nose always goes where the two lines meet.*

*Most cartoon characters have cheeks that stick out more than on real people. Their foreheads are also bigger than normal, especially on wise guys and cute characters.*

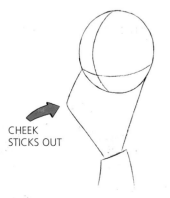

CHEEK
STICKS OUT

SLOPING
FOREHEAD

# ANIMAL HEADS

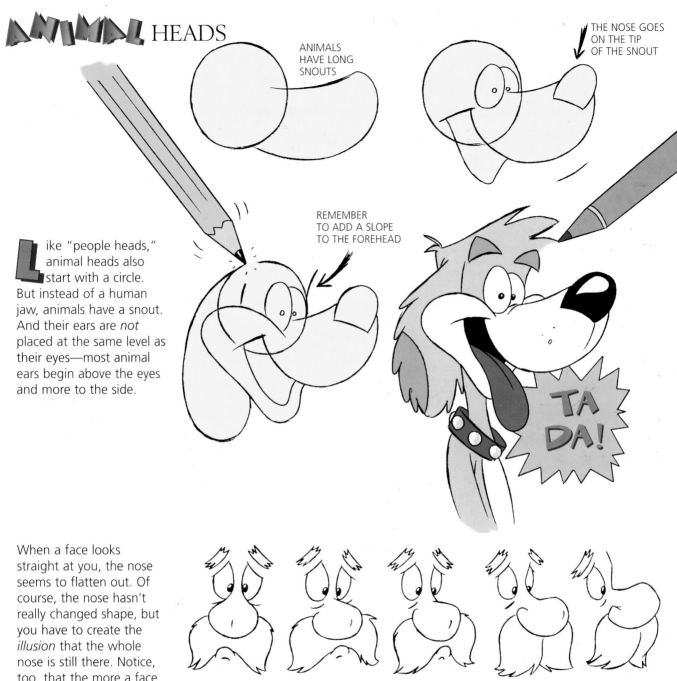

ANIMALS HAVE LONG SNOUTS

THE NOSE GOES ON THE TIP OF THE SNOUT

REMEMBER TO ADD A SLOPE TO THE FOREHEAD

TA DA!

Like "people heads," animal heads also start with a circle. But instead of a human jaw, animals have a snout. And their ears are *not* placed at the same level as their eyes—most animal ears begin above the eyes and more to the side.

When a face looks straight at you, the nose seems to flatten out. Of course, the nose hasn't really changed shape, but you have to create the *illusion* that the whole nose is still there. Notice, too, that the more a face turns away from you, the smaller the *far* eye becomes. This is because it is hidden more and more behind the nose.

FRONT VIEW    SLIGHT SHIFT    3/4 VIEW    NEAR PROFILE    PROFILE

# DRAWING CARTOON WOMEN

**S**ome beginners have difficulty drawing cartoon women. Let's look at the key differences between cartoon men's and women's heads.

| FEATURE | MEN | WOMEN |
| --- | --- | --- |
| EYES | Round | Almond-shaped |
| EYELASHES | Usually none | Thick and long |
| EYEBROWS | Bushy | Thin |
| LIPS | Lower lip is full | Both lips are full |
| JAW | Varies in size | Usually small |
| EARS | Round, large | Small |
| HAIR | Depends on the character | Depends on the character |

*Men usually have squarer faces and chins and thicker eyebrows.*

*Women usually have more oval faces, thinner eyebrows, and smaller (and pointier) chins.*

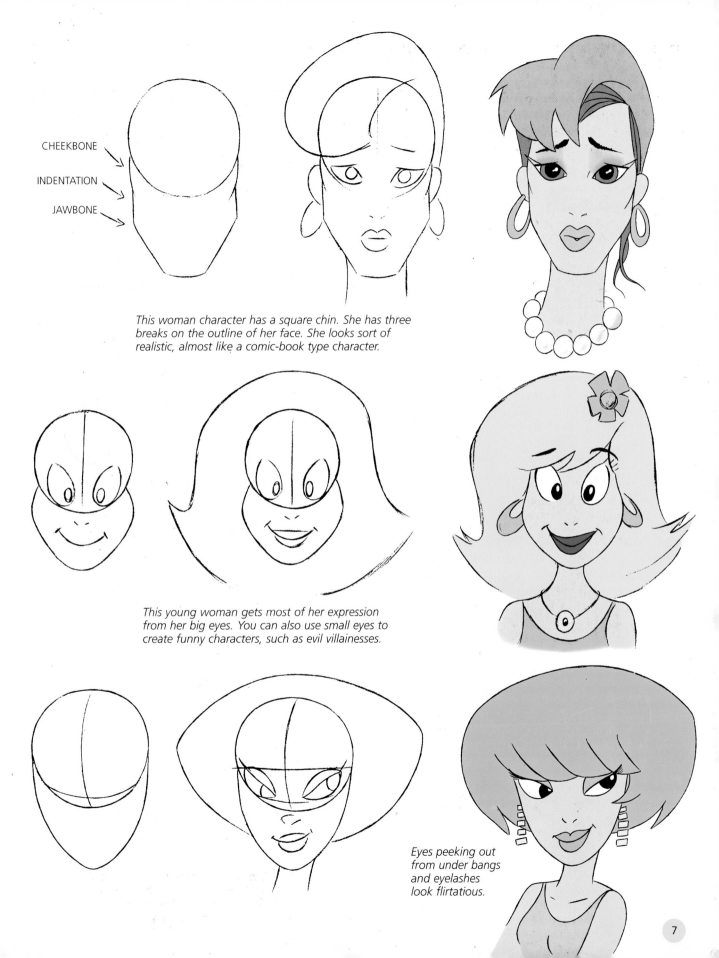

CHEEKBONE

INDENTATION

JAWBONE

This woman character has a square chin. She has three breaks on the outline of her face. She looks sort of realistic, almost like a comic-book type character.

This young woman gets most of her expression from her big eyes. You can also use small eyes to create funny characters, such as evil villainesses.

Eyes peeking out from under bangs and eyelashes look flirtatious.

# THE CENTER LINE

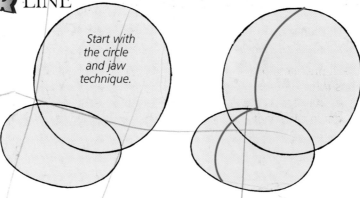

*Start with the circle and jaw technique.*

*Draw a line around the center, as if the two circles were connected balls. This is a 3/4 view.*

The what? The *centerline*. When you draw a head in a front view, it's pretty easy to tell where the center is. But when the head is turned one way or the other, it's harder to find the center. As a result, you might place some of the features a little off-center, and your cartoons will look strangely wrong. Use the centerline to check the features, then you can adjust them if you have to.

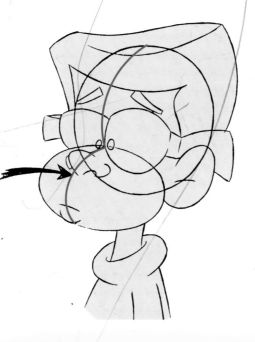

*The nose is placed on the centerline.*

*The finished drawing looks solid.*

*The mouth is off the centerline.*

*In this example, the mouth is wrong. Drawing a centerline can help you fix mistakes like this one.*

# THE CENTERLINE: ANIMALS

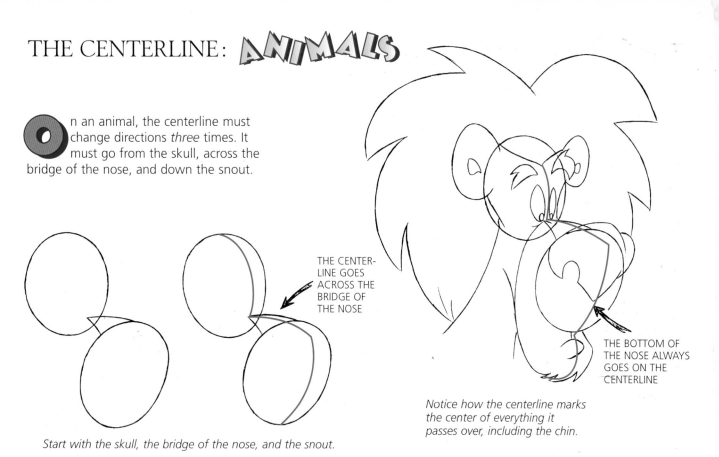

On an animal, the centerline must change directions *three* times. It must go from the skull, across the bridge of the nose, and down the snout.

THE CENTER-LINE GOES ACROSS THE BRIDGE OF THE NOSE

THE BOTTOM OF THE NOSE ALWAYS GOES ON THE CENTERLINE

*Notice how the centerline marks the center of everything it passes over, including the chin.*

*Start with the skull, the bridge of the nose, and the snout.*

THE NOSE IS OFF-CENTER HERE. IT LOOKS WRONG

# BE A CHARACTER DESIGNER!

**F**orget about being a doctor. You want to spend your life having people sneeze on you? Is that really what you want? Be a character designer.

Character design is an important part of any cartoon—from comic strips to animated films. If a character is dull, no one, not even a master animator, can make it lovable. The character needs to be *designed* well to begin with.

So how do you design a new character? Simply by making changes to an old one. Throughout this book, you'll meet characters whose faces and bodies give them personality—such as a "big jaw" that makes a character look "rugged." You can make your own new characters by borrowing physical characteristics like these.

### NICE GUY
*This face is pretty ordinary and round, except that the line in back of the head becomes the line of the back of the neck without an indentation. The smile is drawn low on the face.*

### WIMPY GUY
*This guy has a small chin (or none at all). He has a small mouth and bad posture. And notice how long his face is.*

### RUGGED GUY
*This guy is all jaw. That chin gives him a rugged look (in a silly way). His smile is drawn high up on his cheek. The neck, chest, and shoulders are thick. The posture is good.*

INVENTING YOUR OWN CHARACTERS IS **FUN!** BY MAKING SMALL CHANGES, YOU CREATE NEW CHARACTERS

# HOW TO DRAW THE CARTOON BODY

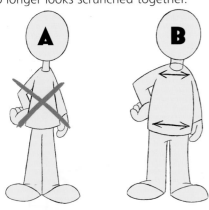

**M**any beginners draw cartoon bodies that don't have any life or energy in them. In Figure A the shoulders and hips are too small. The neck is the size of a toothpick and the legs are too narrow. Figure B is better. The shoulders and hips are wider. It no longer looks scrunched together.

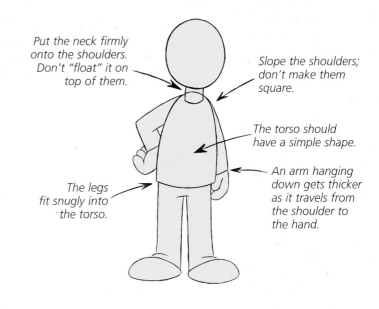

*Put the neck firmly onto the shoulders. Don't "float" it on top of them.*

*Slope the shoulders; don't make them square.*

*The torso should have a simple shape.*

*The legs fit snugly into the torso.*

*An arm hanging down gets thicker as it travels from the shoulder to the hand.*

## BODIES MADE OF SINGLE SHAPES

**A**n easy way to draw a cartoon body is to pick a single shape for the torso and then add arms and legs. This will give you what I call a "stiff" character. The character will have no waist, so although it can move, it cannot bend as naturally as the more advanced bodies on the following pages. But this doesn't mean stiff characters are bad. Their appeal lies in the simpleness of their body shapes.

### FACT!
The body is made up of sections that fit together on hinges we call *joints*.

BEAR/OVAL

MAN/ SQUARE

DANCING DOG/CIRCLE

# BODIES MADE OF TWO CIRCLES

**B**odies that move, twist, and bend, as well as bodies that look more like real humans and animals, are made with two circles. Sometimes these circles overlap. Other times, the circles are connected by two lines.

Bodies built on two circles are better for animation, which is based on movement. Comic strip artists, on the other hand, tend to prefer "stiff" bodies based on a single shape.

HEAD

CHEST AND RIB CAGE

TUMMY AND PELVIS

HEAD

CHEST AND RIB CAGE

HINDQUARTERS

TO DRAW LONG TORSOS, SPACE THE CIRCLES APART

# STIFF BODIES VERSUS BODIES IN MOTION

 stiff body can be stacked, like you would with building blocks. Once the sections are complete and the face is drawn in, you just add the details.

*1. Draw the major sections: head, torso, legs.*

*2. Add arms and sketch in the hands. Start to build the face.*

*3. Place the features on the face and add hair. Draw the fingers. Here's a trick: Draw a collar, and the torso will look like a shirt.*

*4. Finish up.*

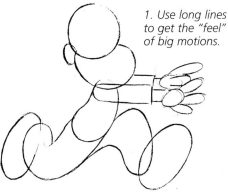

*1. Use long lines to get the "feel" of big motions.*

*2. The facial expression should show the urgency of the pose.*

This runner's body has been built on two circles, even though you can't see them. What you see instead is sort of a pear shape for the torso. A pear is what you get when you draw two overlapping circles and the top circle is smaller than the bottom circle. A pear shape is the cartoonist's shorthand for two overlapping circles.

*3. The cartoon run looks best when there is one unbroken line that flows from one leg to the other in a long stride.*

*4. Tie flapping, glasses left behind— this guy is really moving!*

# DRAWING A STYLIZED CHARACTER

To most people, "style" means a way of drawing, as in an artist's "style." But for cartoonists, a "stylized" cartoon has a very different meaning. Stylizing a cartoon means pushing it past the ordinary, making it a little weird. The purpose is to make the drawing stand out and be daring.

In order to do that, the cartoonist must carefully choose which parts of the character to change. Highly stylized cartoons, such as the Powerpuff Girls, push everything to the breaking point, with hilarious results. But you don't have to go that far to develop a stylized cartoon character.

His hair is fanned out all pointy around his head.

His glasses are much too small.

His tie is ridiculously small.

His waistline is where his chest should be.

His body is just one shape, from his torso to his legs.

His pants are extra wide and long. They almost cover his shoes.

# CHARACTER TYPES BY HEIGHT

Y ou may not be able to tell a book by its cover, but you *can* tell a lot about a character by its *height*. In fact, height helps show a character's personality. Strange but true!

## CARTOONY

Often, cartoony characters are two heads high. These guys are more stylized because there's only room to show simple emotions. Young and cute characters can also be two heads high. Angry little guys, like the one here, also work well at this height.

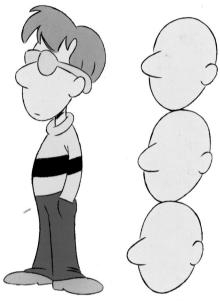

## CLASSIC

Three heads high is about as short as you can be and still get respect as a cartoon character. There's now enough body to bend and stretch and show action poses, but the anatomy has to be pretty simple. Wise guys and Average Joes are typical characters for this height.

## EXCEPTIONS

The exceptions to all this are giant characters, such as monsters and bullies. We draw bullies with small heads and big bodies—they may be five or even six heads tall. Goofy characters who are long and skinny can also go past the four heads mark.

## REALISTIC

At four heads tall, there is enough room to start drawing normal human anatomy. Leading cartoon men and women and their supporting players are best drawn at this height. It becomes more and more difficult to make a character look cartoony when you get to five or six heads tall. (Seven heads tall is, in fact, about normal for actual humans.)

# MORE BODIES

H eight, posture, and shape are three basic things to keep in mind when designing a cartoon character's body.

**CLASSIC VICTIM OR DAD
(SAME THING!)**

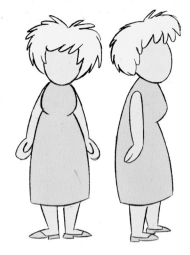

**OVERWORKED MOM**

**LIMITED ANIMATION CHARACTER**

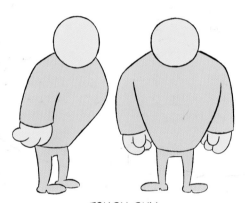

**TOUGH GUY**

**SHORT BULLY**

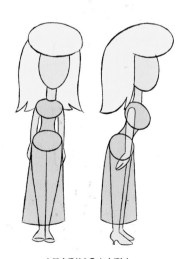

**LEADING LADY**

**GOOFY TYPE**

**MOTHER-IN-LAW**

# THE ACTION LINE

 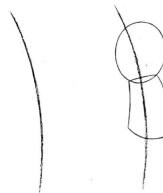 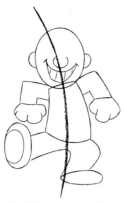 

The *action line* is a single imaginary line that shows the general *sweep* of a character's pose. It gives your drawings more energy. The action line is drawn first, then the character is drawn on top of it. When the character is finished, the action line is erased.

*Draw a line in the general direction you want your character to go.*

*Draw the head and torso on top of the action line.*

*Add the arms and legs, which may or may not be on the action line.*

*Can't you just feel the energy of this character?*

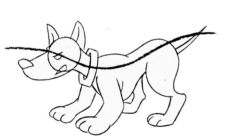

SWIMMING

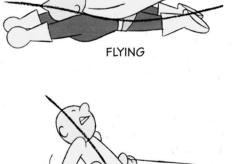

FLYING

GROWLING

WALKING

PULLING

REACHING

THROWING

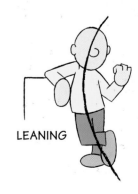

LEANING

17

 QUEEN!

I f there was ever a time for the action line, this is it. The more this skater leans into her pose, the faster she seems to be going. By putting all of her weight over the skates, I've made her look confident, like she knows what she's doing. If I wanted her to look like a beginner, I would show her leaning backward, with her arms flailing. Try it both ways.

*The smoke cloud and the speed lines let you know she's going fast.*

# THE CARTOON

A lot of things happen when you walk. We do these things naturally, so we must take a moment to remember just how we do them. Then we can make our characters do the same.

Notice that when the stride is fully extended, the back leg is usually locked.

*The faster you walk, the more your body tilts forward. As your body tilts forward, your head drops slightly, making you seem shorter. Makes sense so far?*

*As you walk faster, your stride gets longer and your arms swing wider. If your walk is a very determined one, you may also bend your elbows and ball your hands up into fists.*

# THE BODY AND THE CENTER LINE

**J**ust when you thought you were done with the centerline—it's BAAAaaaCK!! By imagining a centerline on the body, you will draw a more correct, round-looking figure.

If you were to draw a cartoon character in a front view—that is, directly facing the reader—then 1/2 of the character's body would be on the left and 1/2 would be on the right. Simple, right? But suppose you turn your character slightly to the right, in a 3/4 view. Then 3/4 of the body is facing the reader and 1/4 of the body is facing away. The centerline can help you show this.

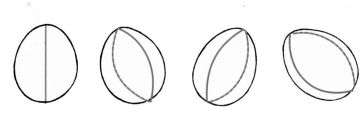

*This guy's body is an egg shape. Try to think of it as a real egg, like one you'd hold in your hand. In the front view, the centerline goes right down the middle. But when we tilt the egg shape, the centerline looks like it's on the side. The centerline travels around the entire surface, even in back where we can't see it, as shown by the dotted lines.*

*You need a centerline to find out where to place a character's buttons and tie.*

Draw a centerline even if something is blocking it (like this guy's hand) to help keep the proportions correct.

Clothing that buttons or zips together, such as on this artist character, comes together on or near the centerline.

This centerline travels from the tiger's face all the way down its massive chest.

Using a centerline will make your characters look rounder and more alive.

# MORE

## NECK TYPES

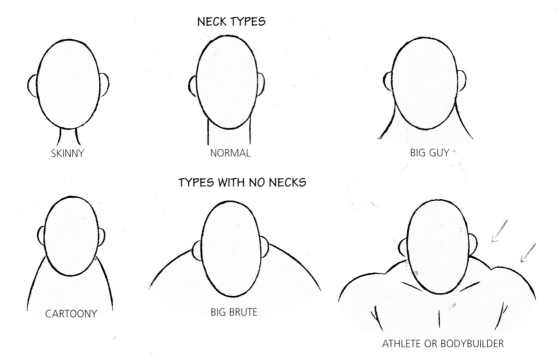

SKINNY

NORMAL

BIG GUY

## TYPES WITH NO NECKS

CARTOONY

BIG BRUTE

ATHLETE OR BODYBUILDER

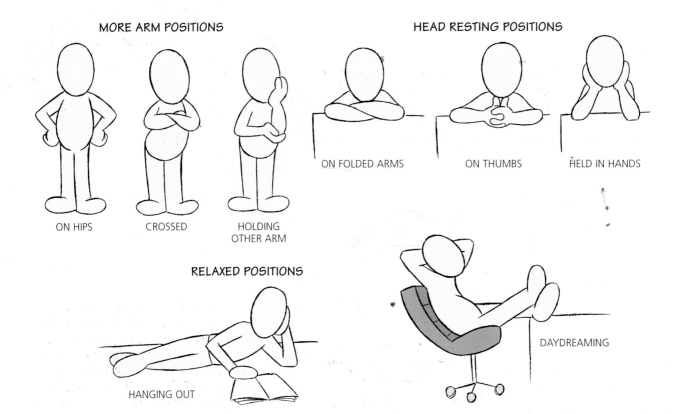

## MORE ARM POSITIONS

ON HIPS

CROSSED

HOLDING
OTHER ARM

## HEAD RESTING POSITIONS

ON FOLDED ARMS

ON THUMBS

HELD IN HANDS

## RELAXED POSITIONS

HANGING OUT

DAYDREAMING

Guy number 1 has only a bathing suit and no props. What can we tell about him? He could be at the beach, or at a pool, but we can't be sure which. He might be running to the water or to the snack bar. He might be a good swimmer or a bad swimmer. We just don't know at this point.

Guy number 2 has a prop. He's wearing fins. Now we can tell more about our character. He is most definitely running to the water. This type of run, with the arms hanging straight down at the sides, makes the character look excited in a silly way.

Guy number 3 has two props: fins and surfboard. The surfboard tells us that, without a doubt, he's at the beach. The fins show that he's probably new at surfing, because most surfers go barefoot. The fins also have another purpose—they make him look goofier. Big feet are always goofy in cartoons.

Guy number 4 is a lifeguard. How do we know this? Look at the whistle around his neck. We know he's goofy from all the stuff he feels he needs to take with him to the water. If you give your character lots of props, you're going to make him look silly—which, as in this case, may be just what you want.

# POPULAR CARTOON PROPS

Cartoon props, like cartoon characters, are simple versions of the real thing. A bit rounder, a bit shorter, a bit funnier, but basically the same. Use as few details as possible to show what the object is.

# MEDIEVAL FOLKS

Costumes are an important part of cartooning, especially when drawing characters from the Dark Ages.

Jesters are always drawn thin and goofy, and never funny enough for the king's taste. One yawn from a bored king sends shivers up the jester's spine.

## TYPES OF CROWNS

LOW WITH RIM

CLASSIC CARTOON

TALL

FANCY

CENTER JEWEL

TIARA

# ROLE VERSUS CHARACTER

A costume tells us what a character's role is, but it doesn't *create* the character. There's a difference. Here are three men whose costumes tell us that they are all prisoners, yet each man has a very different personality. It is not enough to add a costume. You must choose a personality and show it in the face and body.

*Can you tell which of these prisoners is the old timer, which is planning an escape, and which does whatever his "boss" tells him to?*

# NORDIC WARRIOR

Norsemen and Vikings are all the same to cartoonists—big guys with horn hats. Even though Vikings were historically cruel and brutal warriors, many cartoonists have given them lovable personalities. Go figure.

Give your Viking a beard. A Viking without a beard is like Santa Claus with a clean shave.

Most Vikings are thought of as burly, with barrel chests that slope in toward a small waist. But Vikings can also be plump or skinny, any way you want. At right is a typical Viking leader.

*Draw roughly at first, making lots of marks. When you're sure the drawing looks right, trace it over for a clean final drawing.*

# CREEPY AND GOONY

These guys are some of my all-time favorite character types. I used to howl when I'd see Bugs Bunny trying to escape from the Mad Scientist's lair. In fact, I still do. Unlike most guys, I would never put off my work to watch football—just Bugs Bunny.

THICK HEAD

LOW, HEAVY BROW

NO NECK

BAD POSTURE

EVIL HAND GESTURES ARE IMPORTANT!

Here's a mad scientist for you. Notice how deep into the body I've placed the head? Add the features, then place the body on two thin legs.

The wrists are thin but the hands are big.

The back can be hunched.

His clothes should look like they haven't been changed in years!

Towering monsters are always fun to draw. Keep their fists big, for crushing. Everything about them should be huge.

Some goony guys are not even humans, but demons. Keep the body round so it doesn't actually get scary. I like to use dinosaurs for inspiration.

# PREHISTORIC CARTOONS

I f there is one thing to remember about drawing funny prehistoric characters, it is to draw them as ordinary modern people, but dress them in animal skins.

*The single-shape "stiff" body works well for cavepeople. Cavepeople are usually very cartoony so they can be drawn two or three heads high.*

*The costume should always be an animal skin.*

# MOMMA, DON'T LET YOUR CARTOONIST GROW UP TO DRAW COWBOYS

### THE HAIR LINE
*This cowboy has a mustache, but his cheeks are free of whiskers or beards. His nose covers part of the mustache. The mustache covers part of his mouth.*

### MAKING THE MUSTACHE SMILE
*The mustache doubles as an upper lip. It rises for a smile, and turns down for a frown.*

T he best way to tell a cartoon guy from a cartoon cowboy is the ten-gallon hat. There is also the scruffy beard, mustache, or whiskers.

### PROFILE CHEATS
*In a true profile, you only see half of the features: one eye, one ear, one eyebrow, and so on. But in cartoons, we show both sides of the mustache. This is cheating, but it makes it easier to tell what the mustache is.*

### BEARD WITH MUSTACHE
*Sheriffs and gunslingers usually have faces almost totally covered in hair. This makes them look mean.*

### WACKY COWBOYS
*Cowboy characters can also be really funny. For this guy, the mustache and the beard are just one big shape.*

### SQUASHING THE FACE
*When one side of the face is squashed, the other side gets longer. The mustache on the longer side droops down, while the mustache on the scrunched side rises up.*

# THE CARTOON ANIMAL

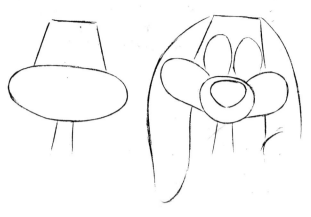

**GOOFY MUTT**
*This guy looks mischievous but cute.*

Certain physical traits create the same personality type for both animals and humans. For instance, goofy humans have hardly any chin—the same with goofy animals. Goofy animals have narrow, sloping shoulders—the same with humans. Goofy animals have thin necks—the same with humans. Goofy animals have long, floppy ears—well, three out of four ain't bad.

**SPACE DOG**
*When you create a character, you need to create a personality for him, too. Space Dog thinks he's from outer space, but he's really just a small dog with a space hat. He loves to scare people by saying there's going to be an invasion from a planet of small, very smart dogs. When Space Dog wants to go out, he tells other dogs in the neighborhood that he's got to take his owner for a walk.*

# CARTOON DOG ANATOMY

This is a realistic-looking cartoon. It's based on the bodies of real dogs.

# ZANY

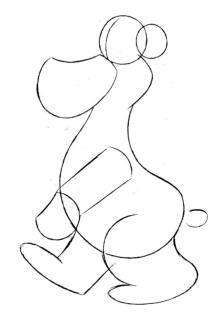

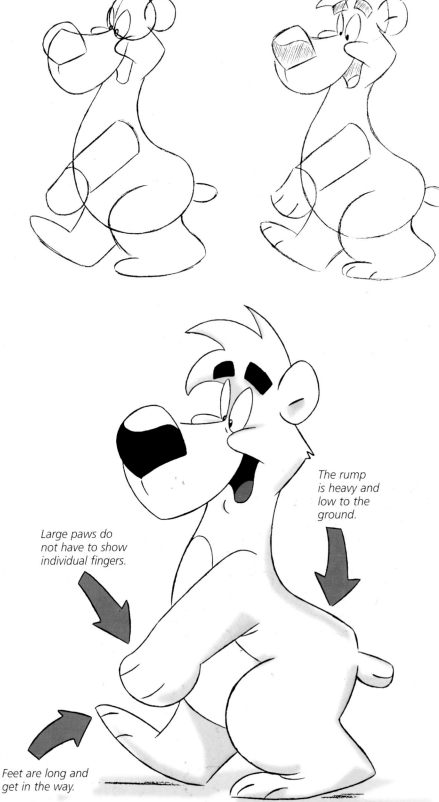

**Z**any characters have a wild, kooky look to them. The eyes seem a little crazy, the mouth is off-center, and the back is heavily arched. Notice that the arm/ shoulder is further forward than it would be on a regular cartoon bear. Making a character zany is one way of stylizing it.

*Large paws do not have to show individual fingers.*

*The rump is heavy and low to the ground.*

*Feet are long and get in the way.*

# OUT OF AFRICA

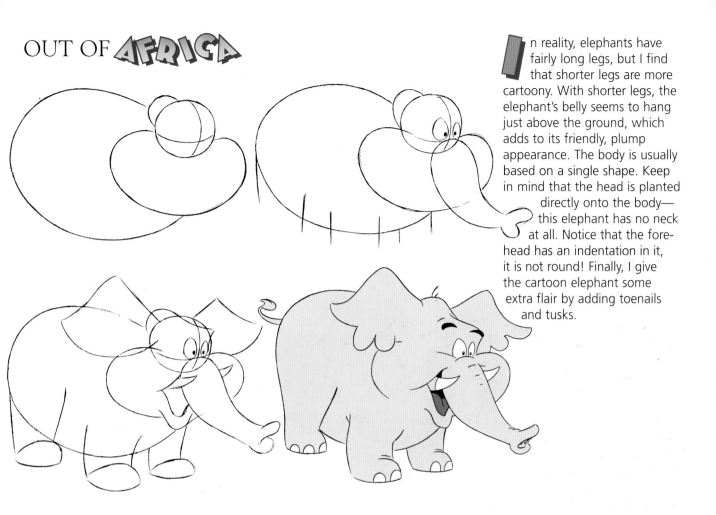

In reality, elephants have fairly long legs, but I find that shorter legs are more cartoony. With shorter legs, the elephant's belly seems to hang just above the ground, which adds to its friendly, plump appearance. The body is usually based on a single shape. Keep in mind that the head is planted directly onto the body— this elephant has no neck at all. Notice that the forehead has an indentation in it, it is not round! Finally, I give the cartoon elephant some extra flair by adding toenails and tusks.

When drawing a lion, you should note that its face is rather long due to its big snout. The forehead is relatively small. Always draw the lion's head *before* adding the mane.

Give your lion a heroic posture: big chest and small hindquarters with a narrow waist. Its paws should be a good size. And, yes, you may now draw the mane.

# MONKEY BUSINESS

SMALL CIRCLE

MEDIUM CIRCLE

LARGE CIRCLE

*The gorilla's head is based on three circles.*

On many gorillas, the eyebrows are connected to form one single eyebrow. This eyebrow is a muscle, which you can use to create expressions.

G orillas are popular cartoon characters because they remind us of ourselves. They probably also remind us of a few relatives.

The gorilla's head can be hard to draw. The reason is that the gorillas's head looks a little like a human head. Many beginners draw an overly human-looking gorilla.

THE EYES AND EARS ARE TINY

THE NECK IS VERY THICK

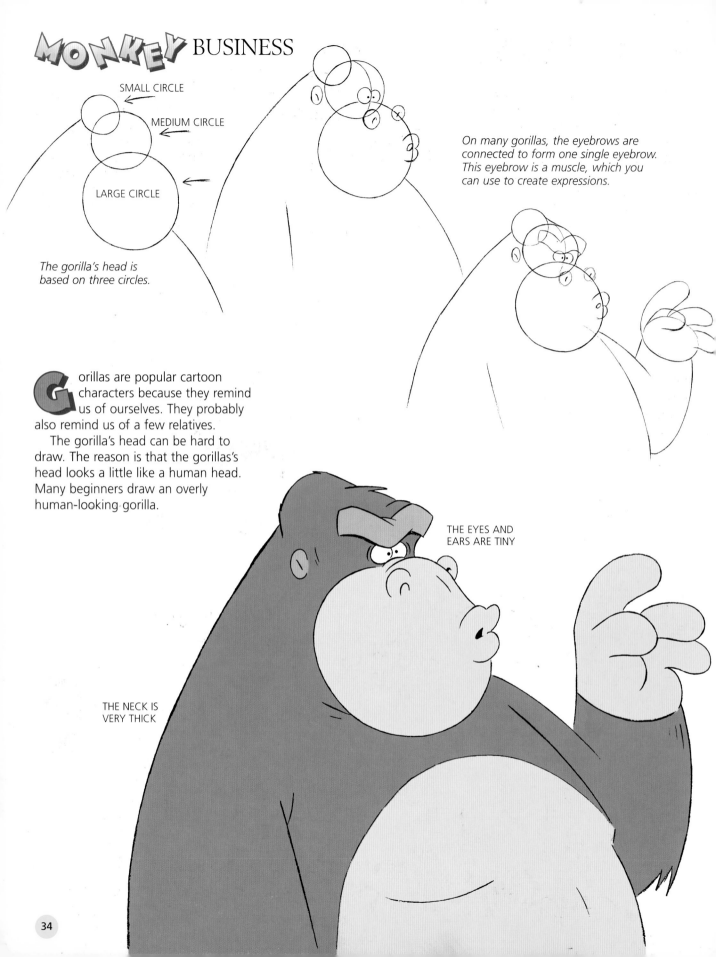

# FOR THE **BIRDS!**

There are so many kinds of birds that no one, except for maybe a bird expert, knows them all. We can therefore take chances in creating unique bird characters.

If you're trying to draw a specific type of bird, however, you've got to be exact. An illustrated encyclopedia of animals can help you get it right.

## KOOKY BIRD
This little fellow is completely imaginary. I don't know of any bird that looks this way. You can mix up parts of different birds to create a unique bird character. All birds, however, share certain qualities that are important to keep. These are:

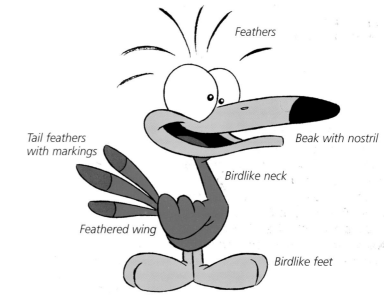

Feathers

Tail feathers
with markings

Beak with nostril

Birdlike neck

Feathered wing

Birdlike feet

## THE PARROT
Here's a popular bird cartoon. The parrot has a hooked beak and fat feet with claws.

Sharp, short, curved beak with small but pronounced chin

Rounded back of head

Long, thick tail feathers

Short, thick legs

Long, grasping feet with large claws

# ADDING THE WORDS

When you create a comic strip, you're working with words as well as with pictures. The expression on your character's face must match his or her words. If a character's words are mild, but her expression is really mad, then the reader won't know which is the character's true mood.

A *dialogue balloon* shows what a character is *saying*. A *thought balloon* (or *thought cloud*) shows what a character is *thinking*. A character's mouth does not have to be open while he or she is speaking (although it usually is). A character's mouth is almost *never* open when he or she is thinking.

Because comic strips in newspapers are so small, it's best to use as few words as possible. We've all seen comic strips that have too many words. The typical reader will just move on to another strip. The crowded strip looks like too much work to read.

# DIALOGUE BALLOONS

Just as there are different styles of cartoons, there are different styles of dialogue balloons. Cartoonists work hard to design new types of dialogue balloons for their strips. Some have no balloons at all, just a line drawn from the dialogue to the character. Look at the comics section of your newspaper to see all different kinds of dialogue balloons.

Some dialogue balloons are used for special effects. These should be used only once in a while, so they have more impact.

*The part of the dialogue balloon that points to the character is called the "pointer." No matter where the dialogue balloon is placed, the pointer should always point at the speaking character's head. Pointers should be kept short.*

### TYPES OF DIALOGUE BALLOONS

OLD-FASHIONED

SMOOTH

RECTANGULAR

RECTANGULAR THOUGHT BALLOON

### SPECIAL-EFFECT BALLOONS

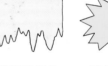
ICY THOUGHT

SPLASH BALLOON (FOR WORDS LIKE POW! AND ZAP!)

PANEL TO INTRODUCE A SCENE ("ONE HOUR LATER...")

### WRITING THE DIALOGUE

Try to write dialogue that adds personality to your cartoon. For example, suppose you want to show a teacher introducing herself to her class. You could have her say "Hello everybody." But that doesn't tell us anything about the teacher's character. If you changed her greeting to "Pay Attention!" we would know more about her. And what's more, we would know she was going to be funny. The same thing goes for the preppies below.

# ADVANCED TECHNIQUES

nce you have practiced the basics, try these more advanced techniques.

*Characters do not have to face each other to have a conversation. One character could have his back turned, walking away as he speaks. Or a character could be in the middle of an action as she speaks. Try to find interesting ways to draw your characters so they're not always standing still when they're talking.*

**CARTOON CONVERSATIONS**
The character speaking first always goes on the left.

## STAGGERING DIALOGUE BALLOONS
I said, he said, I said. That's about as much as you can fit in a cartoon panel. Three lines of dialogue, back and forth. More than that and you'd better write a book instead.

*You can stack dialogue balloons between the characters. It's clear and easy to read. The problem is that the balloons block the background.*

*If you put the dialogue balloons overhead, you can see the background. There is also better eye contact between the characters.*

## VOICE VOLUME
Different lettering styles can make a character's voice seem louder or softer.

REGULAR LETTERING SHOWS A PERSON CALLING

BOLD LETTERING SHOWS SHOUTING

HEAVY BLOCK LETTERING SHOWS YELLING

RED BLOCK LETTERS SHOW SCREAMING!

# CREATING MORE  FOR DIALOGUE BALLOONS

 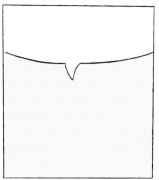

**A** dialogue balloon takes up a lot of space in your comic strip panel. One way to get more room is to have the top of your panel cut off the top of the dialogue balloon.

Every once in a while you can "break the panel." This is when the dialogue balloon goes over into the next panel. It's best to do this only once in each comic strip. Otherwise, the strip will start to look messy.

Here's another technique. Draw the dialogue balloon within the panel, with the pointer *cut off* by the border. This makes it look as though the speaker is outside the panel. The next panel should be drawn as a new panel, with the characters in new positions.

You can also get more space by placing the character in *front* of the dialogue balloon. (Don't place him in back or he'll be partly hidden by the balloon.)

# DESIGNING A PANEL

If a farmer is traveling fifty miles an hour for forty miles, how many bushels of corn does he have? Man, I hated those questions! Cartoonists never have to answer questions like that.

But here's the catch. You *do* have to answer a question just as hard each time you begin to draw a new panel: How am I going to design this scene? Here are a few basic rules to help you.

*Characters who are supposed to be near the reader should be farther away from the horizon line.*

HORIZON LINE

HORIZON LINE

*Characters who are supposed to look far away should be close to the horizon line.*

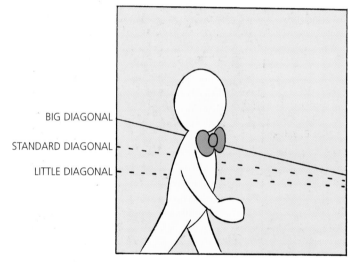

BIG DIAGONAL

STANDARD DIAGONAL

LITTLE DIAGONAL

*To add drama to a scene, make the horizon line a diagonal. The greater the diagonal, the more tension in your scene. Be careful, though, because you can overdo it.*

*To show depth, you can draw the corner of a room in two ways:*

*Draw a corner of the floor (leave out the ceiling).*

*Draw a corner of the ceiling (leave out the floor).*

# ADVANCED LAYOUTS

*Props in the front of a scene (the "foreground") work best in the corner. This way, they won't get in the way of the main scene.*

FOREGROUND CORNER

FOREGROUND CORNER

*The same goes for people—if they are in the foreground and they're not important for the scene, put them in the corner.*

BACKGROUND

*Layer the scene to create depth.*

SUBJECT

FOREGROUND

*A running character is best placed in the middle of the page.*

*To show people riding in cars, "long shots" are best. Long shots leave plenty of room for dialogue balloons.*

# COMIC STRIP JOKES
# AND CHARACTER IDEAS

L et's get started! I want you to get the instant fun of putting together a comic strip, so I've supplied some joke and character ideas for you. If you have your own jokes and characters, that's great, too.

As you can see, comic strip scripts are laid out panel by panel. Each panel sets up the next one. Try to think visually. Approach each panel as a new problem to be solved. But also remember that, in the end, all of the panels must flow together.

## JOKE #1

PANEL 1: A 16-year-old girl (TARA) approaches her brainy younger brother (ALBERT), who is happily working at his computer. Tara carries her schoolbooks, and looks frustrated.

TARA: "Albert, I need help with my homework."

PANEL 2: ALBERT turns off the computer and pays attention to his sister.

ALBERT: "Show me what the problem is and I'll explain it to you."

PANEL 3: TARA tosses the books into Albert's lap, turns around and walks off. ALBERT looks confused.

TARA: "Spare me the explanations! Just call me when you're done!"

## JOKE #2

PANEL 1: A BOY is standing in his room, gazing at the stars through a telescope. His MOTHER walks in.

BOY: "I predict that someday, man will travel through the vastness of space to a new solar system!"

PANEL 2: MOTHER comments about the messy room.

MOM: "He's not going to get there unless he first learns how to straighten his room."

PANEL 3: The MOTHER is gone from the panel. The BOY comments to the reader as he picks up his clothes.

BOY: "It's amazing how many opportunities she can find to say that."

## JOKE #3

PANEL 1: Overhead sign reads: MATERNITY WARD. An EXPECTANT FATHER and MOTHER arrive. A NURSE comments to them.

NURSE: "The woman in room 509 just had triplets."

PANEL 2: A DIALOGUE BALLOON streams into the panel from down the hallway.

DIALOGUE BALLOON: "WAAAAAA!!!!!"

PANEL 3: EXPECTANT FATHER: "What a loud cry that baby has."

PANEL 4: The NURSE replies as she calmly walks past. The EXPECTANT FATHER reacts.

NURSE: "That's the husband."

## JOKE #4

PANEL 1: THE SCHOOL CAFETERIA. THE BULLY approaches a SHY KID who is eating his lunch alone.

BULLY: "My mom says I gotta learn how to share."

PANEL 2: The SHY KID is relieved.

SHY KID: "That's a good idea."

PANEL 3: The BULLY yanks the SHY KID out of his chair, and sits down in front of the SHY KID'S food.

BULLY: "So let's start by sharing your lunch."

## JOKE #5

PANEL 1: A TEENAGE GIRL talks on the phone while her YOUNG BROTHER listens.

TEENAGE GIRL: "Bobby Lazer asked me out tonight."

PANEL 2: Same scene.

TEENAGE GIRL: "But my mother is making me stay home to babysit my kid brother instead."

PANEL 3: The YOUNGER BROTHER looks at the reader, worried, and comments to reader in a thought balloon.

YOUNGER BROTHER: "Why do I get this feeling of impending doom?"

## JOKE #6

PANEL 1: KNIGHT #1 is engaged in a vicious sword fight with KNIGHT #2. Their swords clash.

SOUND EFFECT: CLANG!

PANEL 2: KNIGHT #2 advances on KNIGHT #1.

SOUND EFFECT: PING!

PANEL 3: KNIGHT #1 advances on KNIGHT #2.

SOUND EFFECT: SMASH!

PANEL 4: Reveal that we're in a medieval sword shop. The sign reads: YE OLDE SWORDS & THINGS. KNIGHT #2 appears behind the cash register. KNIGHT #1 is holding and admiring the sword.

KNIGHT #1: "I'LL TAKE IT!"

## JOKE #7

A MOTHER BIRD is feeding worms to the CHICKS in her nest. One of the chicks looks at the reader and comments—

CHICK: "The worm part is bad enough, but when she chews it for me first, it really blows my appetite."

## JOKE #8

PANEL 1: A BEAR is being examined in a DOCTOR'S office.

BEAR: "Doc, I got insomnia."

DOC: "How bad is it?"

PANEL 2: Same scene.

BEAR: "I can only sleep for five months out of the year."

# DRAW YOUR OWN COMIC STRIP

Just photocopy the blank comic strip panels that follow and you can draw as many comic strips as you want! Copy them at 200 percent, which means that you're making them twice their original size.

# ANIMATION!

**T**he word *animation* means *magic*. So does the word *abracadabra*, but what I'm going to show you is lots more fun than watching a guy pour milk into a rolled-up newspaper.

ENDING EXTREME

BEGINNING EXTREME

BREAKDOWN DRAWING

PLACE THE IN-BETWEENS HERE

Animators create the illusion of movement by using a series of drawings that flow from one to the next. To animate a motion, draw the starting point of the move and the ending point—these are called the *extremes*. Then find the halfway point between the extremes and draw that. This is called the *breakdown* drawing. The drawings between the breakdown and the extremes are called *in-betweens*. Those are drawn last. Why do animators work this way, rather than simply starting at the beginning and working their way to the end? Because it's easy to lose your way through so many drawings. You might begin to change the character, and by the time the movement ended, the character wouldn't look the same as when it started.

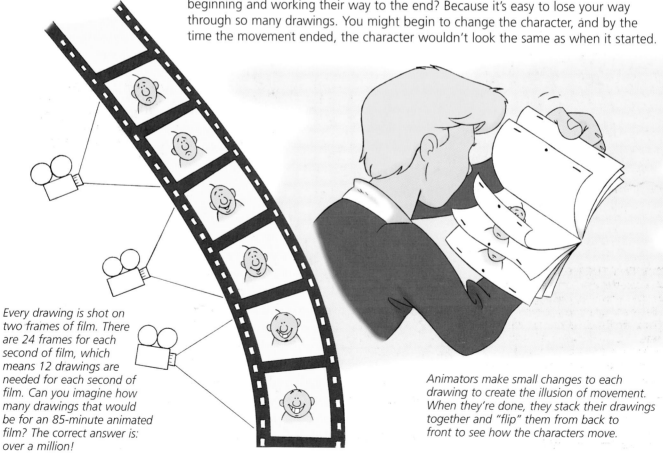

*Every drawing is shot on two frames of film. There are 24 frames for each second of film, which means 12 drawings are needed for each second of film. Can you imagine how many drawings that would be for an 85-minute animated film? The correct answer is: over a million!*

*Animators make small changes to each drawing to create the illusion of movement. When they're done, they stack their drawings together and "flip" them from back to front to see how the characters move.*

# THE RULES OF MOTION

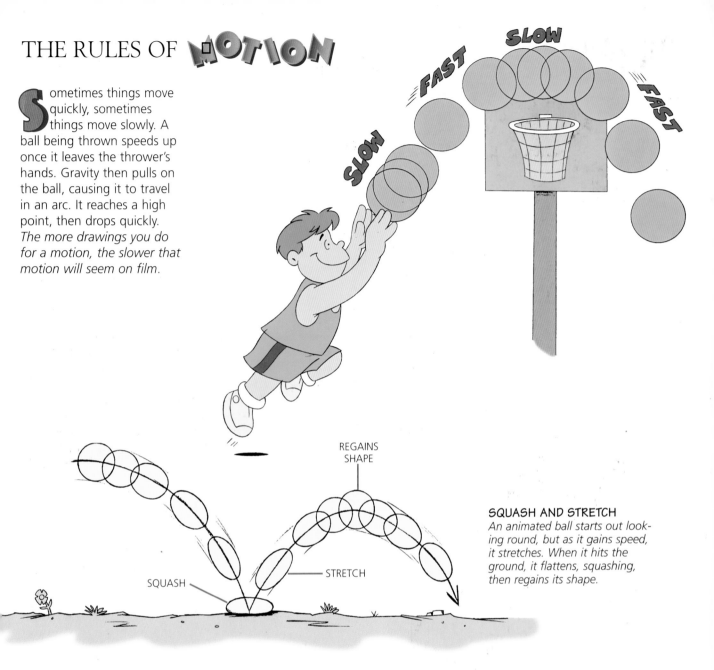

**S**ometimes things move quickly, sometimes things move slowly. A ball being thrown speeds up once it leaves the thrower's hands. Gravity then pulls on the ball, causing it to travel in an arc. It reaches a high point, then drops quickly. *The more drawings you do for a motion, the slower that motion will seem on film.*

SLOW · FAST · SLOW · FAST

REGAINS SHAPE

SQUASH

STRETCH

## SQUASH AND STRETCH
*An animated ball starts out looking round, but as it gains speed, it stretches. When it hits the ground, it flattens, squashing, then regains its shape.*

## TURNING THE HEAD
*Animated characters are always in motion—turning, twisting, tilting. Here's an experiment for you. Draw the heads as you see them here. The ones on the left and right are extremes. The middle head is the breakdown. Then draw two in-between drawings, one to go between the first and second drawings, another to go between the second and third drawings. Then flip all five drawings to see if they animate smoothly.*

# CYCLES

To create animation, you must keep your drawings in *register*, which means that you must start each drawing at the same spot on each page. You can't draw your character at the bottom of the first page, the top of the second page, and the middle of the next page—that would make him seem to jump around.

To keep your drawings in register, draw a small "X" on the upper-left and lower-right sides of each page. Trace the "X" on as many sheets of paper as you think you will need. (Trace your "X"s from your originally marked page only.) Before you start a new drawing, line up the X's with those on the last drawing you did. Now your drawing will be in register.

A *cycle* is a movement that starts at A, goes to B, C, D, E, then starts all over again at A. A cycle can keep going forever. There are run cycles, walk cycles, and flying cycles (for birds). Almost any motion can be turned into a cycle if it ends exactly where it began.

The cartoon walk may seem simple, but it isn't. When you walk, every part of your body is in constant motion, even your hips and shoulders. When you walk, you are also constantly changing heights.

THE WALK CYCLE

**THINKING AN ACTION THROUGH**
*Suppose you want your character to jump in the air. It takes more than just drawing a character going up and down. First, the character anticipates the jump by going in the opposite direction.*

*Next, she stretches as she leaps into the air. As gravity pulls on her she slows down.*

*As she comes back down, she picks up speed. She squashes as she lands, then she recovers. Notice, too, how her ears and tail drag behind, reacting to the motion a bit late.*